THE FIRE OF LONDON

RUPERT MATTHEWS

Illustrated by Richard Scollins

The Bookwright Press
New York · 1989

Great Disasters

The Chernobyl Catastrophe
The Hindenburg Tragedy
The Eruption of Krakatoa
The Fire of London

The Destruction of Pompeii
The San Francisco Earthquake
The Space Shuttle Disaster
The Sinking of the Titanic

Front cover: A seventeenth-century picture of the fire entitled "London's feir began September the Second, 1666."

First published in the
United States in 1989 by
The Bookwright Press
387 Park Avenue South
New York, NY 10016

First published in 1988 by
Wayland (Publishers) Ltd
61 Western Road, Hove
East Sussex BN3 1JD, England

Typeset by Direct Image Photosetting,
Burgess Hill, East Sussex
Printed in Italy by G. Canale & C.S.p.A., Turin

Words that are printed in **bold** the first time they appear in the text are explained in the glossary.

Library of Congress Cataloging-in-Publication
Matthews, Rupert.
  The fire of London.

  (Great disasters)
  Bibliography: p.
  Includes index.
  Summary: Presents a historical, partly fictional, account of the Great Fire of London in 1666, describing the origins, fire fighting methods, effects on people, and rebuilding efforts.
  Contrasts London then and the city now in the areas of population, housing and world trade.
  1. London (England)— History—17th century—Juvenile literature. 2. Fires—England—London —History—17th century—Juvenile literature. [1. Fires—England—London. 2. London (England)—History—17th century] I. Scollins, Richard, ill. II. Title. III. Series.
DA681.M38   1989   942.1'2066   88-5054
ISBN 0-531-18237-1

CONTENTS

Flames at Night   4

A Great City   8

The First Spark   12

Fighting the Fire   16

Refugees   24

Future Plans   26

Glossary   30

Books to Read   31

Further Information   31

Index   32

FLAMES AT NIGHT

"It was Mr. Jenkins, my master goldsmith, who woke me up," said Tom. "He shook me by the shoulder in the middle of the night. I looked round but it was dark. 'Hurry, Tom,' he said, 'the street's on fire. We'll have to leave.'

"It took me a bit of time to realize what was going on. Mr. Jenkins left the room telling me to follow him. I got dressed as quickly as I could and went downstairs. As soon as I reached the shop, I could see the flames. The house opposite was on fire.

"I moved to the window but Mr. Jenkins called me back. 'Come on Tom,' he said, 'it's time you earned your keep as an **apprentice**.' He was busy packing all our stock into sacks.

Mr. Jenkins filled two sacks with jewelry and gold scraps. He gave one to me and then we left the shop.

"The scene in the street was amazing. Up the hill, the whole street was on fire. Red flames were leaping around every house and shop. Sparks whirled up into the sky, like a thousand stars. For a moment I stood staring at the horrific scene, but then Mr. Jenkins pulled my shirt and pushed me down the hill.

"We ran toward the river. Mr. Jenkins hoped that there would be a boat to take us across. A troop of the **trained bands** marched past us toward the fire. They were armed with buckets and **squirts**. I didn't think they could do much against the fire, but at least they were trying.

Tom and Mr. Jenkins found themselves in a street full of burning red flames. Frightened people were leaving their homes with their belongings.

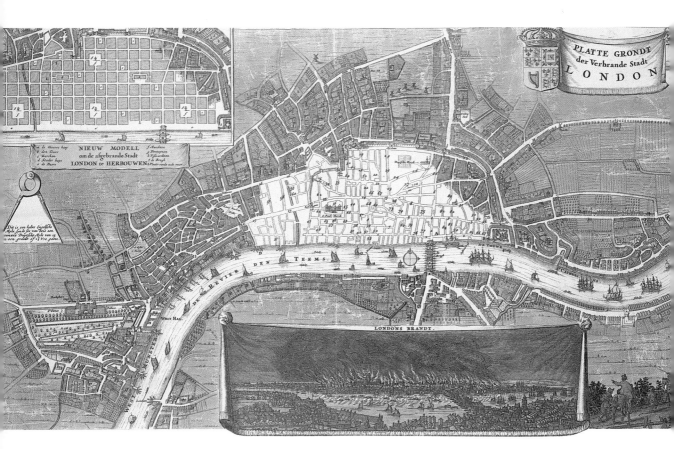

NIEUW MODELL
om de afgebrande Stadt
LONDON te HERBOUWEN

DE REVIER DEN TEEMS.

WIT HAL

LONDONS BRANDT.

"We hurried through Philpot Lane toward Botolph Lane. People were leaving their houses. Some people ran out screaming in fright. Others were trying to save their property from the flames. They were carrying sacks, just like Mr. Jenkins and myself. One man had even found a horse and cart somewhere. He was loading his bed and other furniture onto it. The horse looked frightened by the flames. I remember thinking that the man would be lucky if the horse didn't bolt.

"The fire seemed to be all around us. It was leaping from building to building in the wind. Just as we reached Thames

Above *A map of London after the fire. The white area at the center of the map shows the area destroyed by the fire.*

Street, a house collapsed behind us. It made a terrible crash as it came down. Then we were beside the river.

"There were hundreds of people by the river, all trying to get into boats. The whole scene was lit by the red glow of the flames behind us. It was the most frightful thing I have ever seen. A **ferryman** came up close to us. Mr. Jenkins held out a handful of coins to him and we climbed into the boat.

6

"The man rowed us across to Bermondsey. Once there, we were safe. The flames never crossed the river."

This is how the Fire of London would have appeared to one of the many apprentices in the city at the time.

Right *Ferrymen helped people flee from the fire by taking them across the Thames.*

Below *A map of 1666, showing Pudding Lane (spelled "Puding"), Philpot Lane and Botolph Lane.*

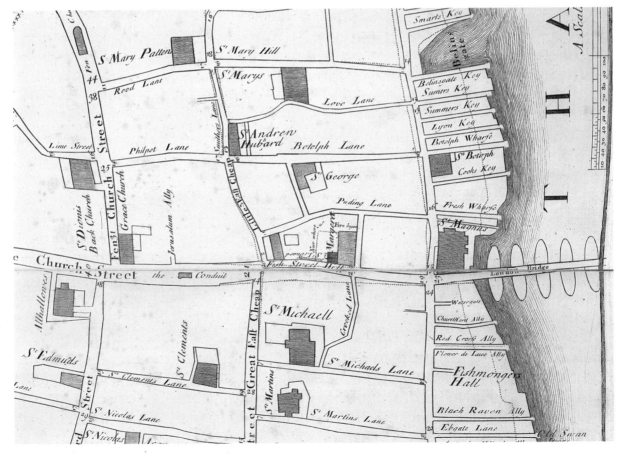

A GREAT CITY

In the summer of 1666, London was by far the largest and most important city in Britain. It was also a major world city. The streets were always busy, by day or night. Rich noblemen and women strolled in the more fashionable areas, and wealthy merchants made deals in coffee shops and at the **Royal Exchange**. The poorer areas were alive with tradesmen and workers who made a living in more humble ways. It was a lively and exciting place.

London then covered a much smaller area than it does today. Islington, for instance, was a quiet country village in 1666. Today it is a busy district of London. The main part of London was then to be found on the north side of the Thames River within the old city walls, in what is now the business area known as the "City." Beyond these walls, houses, palaces and churches stretched westward to Westminster. Along the riverbanks to the east of the city stretched docks and warehouses.

It was from these docks that the ships of the London merchants set sail. They traveled all over the known world.

Above right *The Royal Exchange, which was destroyed when "the fire ran around the galleries."*

Below *A seventeenth-century painting of London Bridge before the fire.*

London ships carried goods to every important port in Europe, from Sweden to Naples, in Italy. The more adventurous captains took their ships to other continents. The colonies in America were thriving. Every year more people wanted to go and live in the "New World." Those already in America needed ships to carry goods such as tobacco back to Europe.

A few ships sailed eastward to India and China. In these far countries, the sailors found rich silks and spices of which most people had only dreamed. The wealth and luxury of all these lands poured back into London.

London was, of course, the capital of Britain. King Charles II held court at Whitehall. The important noblemen and members of Parliament had homes in London. They traveled through the streets in magnificent coaches and wore expensive clothes.

But the streets of London were very different from those of today. They were narrow and dirty. The houses and stores were packed closely together. Some streets were so narrow that they were little more than alleyways. Each story of the wooden buildings projected over the one below. The upper stories of some buildings nearly met across the street.

Almost all houses were built of wood. Large, thick timbers supported the walls and floors. Thinner strips of wood covered with **daub** formed the walls. The summer of 1666 was long and hot. By autumn the city of London was **tinder** dry. The wooden buildings would have gone up in flames from the smallest spark. On the night of September 2, that spark was struck.

Above *This engraving shows the dark, narrow streets of London.*

Left *Houses built at the time of the fire had wooden beams, with walls made out of strips of wood (wattles) covered with plaster (daub).*

THE FIRST SPARK

Among the many thriving businesses in London in 1666 was a baker's shop belonging to a man called John Farynor. The shop stood in Pudding Lane, a narrow street close to London Bridge. Every morning, Farynor and his workers mixed dough, stoked their ovens with fresh wood and baked bread. Farynor sold some of his bread to the Royal Palace and was known as the King's Baker.

Because he needed to keep his ovens at a steady, high temperature, Farynor kept large stocks of **faggots** of dry wood in his kitchen. At two o'clock on the morning of September 2 these stocks of wood caught fire. At the time, some people said Farynor was a careless man and that he did not take precautions against fire. However, we do not know the truth, and the fire may have been a genuine accident.

The fire was discovered by one of Farynor's servants. The flames spread rapidly and soon the ground floor of the bakery was alight. Farynor and his household had to escape by climbing onto the roof and jumping across to the next house. One of the maids refused to risk the leap. She stayed in the bakery and was burned to death.

The flames spread with frightening speed. By the time John Farynor had awakened his neighbors, his whole bakery was on fire. Though people did what they could with buckets of water, the flames quickly spread along Pudding Lane. By dawn dozens of houses in the area were on fire.

John Farynor and his family escaped the flames by jumping to the roof of a neighboring house.

As soon as the **watchmen** realized that the flames were getting out of control, they woke up Sir Thomas Bludworth, the **Lord Mayor** of London. Bludworth hurried to the scene to try to organize the fire-fighting. A strong east wind was blowing, fanning the flames, which leaped from house to house. The fire's relentless rush forward was terrifying. It raced down toward the river and moved west through the city.

Samuel Pepys, whose diary became famous, was then an important government official. He realized how dangerous the fire was becoming. He hurried to Whitehall to tell King Charles. The King sent a message to Bludworth offering to send soldiers to help fight the flames. Bludworth accepted the offer.

By late afternoon, the situation was rapidly getting out of control. Bludworth was still trying to defeat the flames, but panic was spreading. Citizens of London who had gathered to help Bludworth now became fearful that the flames would burn their own houses. They abandoned Bludworth and ran back to try to rescue valuables

Above *Samuel Pepys recorded the events of the fire in his famous diary.*

Above *An engraving from a book showing people trying to save their possessions from the flames.*

Left *A magnificent painting of the fire. In the center, old St. Paul's Cathedral can be seen burning.*

from their homes before the flames engulfed them too. Soon Bludworth was almost alone. He sadly turned away. The fire raged out of control.

The houses on London Bridge caught fire and blocked the roadway. By the time evening fell on September 2, hundreds of houses and dozens of churches had been destroyed, and many more were in flames. It seemed that nothing could stop the fire.

FIGHTING THE FIRE

All through the hot Sunday night, the fire continued to rage. It swept down to the **warehouses** along the riverside. As the tall wooden buildings caught fire, the blaze took on a terrible new aspect.

The warehouses were packed with a wide variety of goods. One was full of exotic spices. The smoke from this building was **acrid** with the stench of burning peppers. Anyone who came

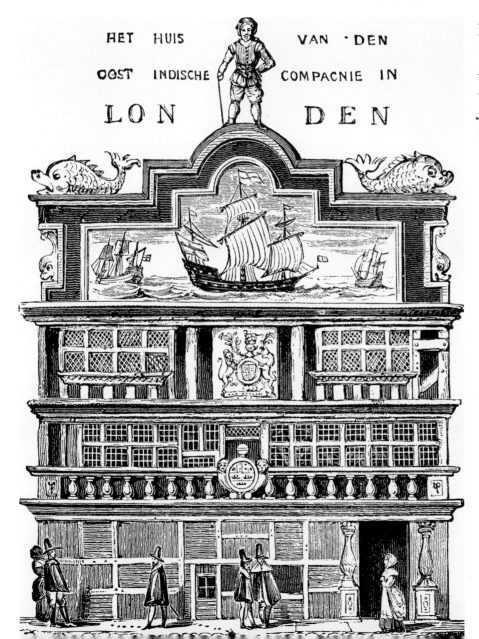

Right (inset) *The docks of London, which had burned so fiercely during the fire.*

Left *East India House on the banks of the Thames. Owned by the Dutch East India Company, this building and warehouse managed to survive the fire.*

close collapsed in the choking fumes. Another warehouse held stores of metal. As it blazed, the metal melted and began to flow out of the building and through the streets like a burning river. Eventually it plunged into the Thames, where it started the river water boiling with the heat.

Below *A hand-operated water pump is used to fight the fire.*

Other warehouses held barrels of brandy and hard liquor. As the barrels split open in the heat, streams of flaming spirits gushed out of the doors and windows. The burning of the warehouses and their contents may well have been the most frightening part of the fire.

When the sun rose on the morning of Monday September 3, the people of London found they could barely see their city. A huge black cloud of smoke and soot almost blotted out the whole sky. Only the leaping, red flames continued to provide some light to fight the fire by.

Below *News of the fire caused a sensation in Europe. This German print shows the interest the fire created in that country. A huge black cloud, created by all the burning warehouse goods, hangs over the city.*

Left People of London huddle under a bridge for safety as they watch the fire spread. Soon the flames would reach St. Paul's Cathedral in the background.

The King intervenes

Word was taken to the King that the fire was still raging out of control. Charles at once called together the **Privy Council** and began issuing orders. Special "Fire Posts" were established throughout the city. Fire-fighting equipment was sent to these posts, together with food and drink. London citizens were asked to gather at the Fire Posts to be organized into efficient work parties. Soldiers were sent to help with the work, and the Trained Bands were called out and given tasks to perform. The Trained Bands were a kind of **militia**. Their members were ordinary Londoners who practiced with weapons in case they were needed to defend London in time of war. King Charles now ordered them to protect London from the fire.

Right *The job of a watchman in the seventeenth century was to guard the city from crime. Such men helped in the fire-fighting.*

Finally, King Charles placed his brother, the Duke of York, in charge of operations. It was decided to try to stop the fire at the **Fleet River**, which then ran through the city. The flimsy wooden **wharves** along the Fleet were demolished. The houses along either side of the river were pulled down. By destroying these wooden structures, it was hoped that the flames could be stopped by starving them of fresh fuel. Unfortunately, the strong east wind brought the flames to the Fleet before the work was completed. The flames easily leaped across the narrow river and continued their destruction.

Within a few hours some of the most magnificent buildings in the city were destroyed. St. Paul's Cathedral went up in flames, as did the Royal Exchange, the Guildhall and Bridewell. Bridewell was completely destroyed by the fire; it was a catastrophic blow, as this was where London's store of grain was kept.

The devastation continues

Though the fire-fighting was now more organized, the fire continued to spread throughout Monday and the following night. Early on Tuesday morning King Charles came with his personal guard to inspect the fire's progress.

The drastic decision was taken to start destroying houses with gunpowder. A **fire-break** had to be established somehow, and gunpowder seemed the only answer. The Duke of York, with the guards, began methodically to demolish houses in a band across London.

The flimsy, wooden wharves and warehouses around the Fleet River in London were pulled down to starve the fire of fresh fuel. Unfortunately, a strong wind spread the flames before the fire-break was completed.

While the steady thunder of explosives rocked London, King Charles rode around the city. He threw himself energetically into the work of fire-fighting, and it encouraged the fire-fighters to see the King so involved in all the efforts to try to stop the fire. At particularly vital spots King Charles would leap from his horse and dash

Above *A type of water pump used to fight the fire.*
Below *A fire-fighter's leather helmet.*

Below *A leather bucket, used to carry water to put out the fire.*

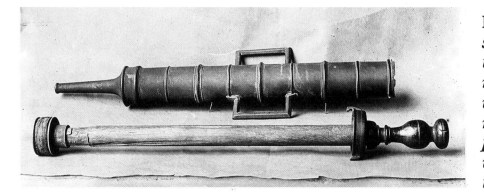

Left *A fire squirt used in the fire. The nozzle (above) was held by two men, as the pump was worked by a third man.*

The Duke of York, King Charles II's brother, directed the fire-fighters.

toward the flames. By carrying buckets of water or using a squirter, the King showed how important such work was. If Charles noticed someone working hard, he would race over and press a golden **guinea** into their hand. Charles kept up this hectic pace for thirty hours without sleep. It is certain that his example encouraged Londoners to continue fighting the flames.

Eventually, on Wednesday September 5, the fire was brought under control. The strong wind dropped, which meant that the flames were no longer so intense. The fire-break blasted through the city by the Duke of York held the flames back. The tireless work of the fire-fighting parties gradually put out the fire.

That evening, Londoners were able to rest and gaze at their shattered city. About four-fifths of it had been burned to the ground. More than 13,000 houses and 87 churches had gone. In all, over 400 acres of the finest city in Britain had been destroyed.

REFUGEES

During the hectic days of the fire, people had no time to think. They had to flee from the flames with whatever goods they could carry away. Many then returned to the city to help fight the flames. It was only when the fire had died down that people could consider their own situations.

Despite the massive destruction caused by the fire, only nine people had died. This was because most people had had enough time to escape. However, more than 100,000 people had lost their homes. The majority of these settled on Moorfields, which was then just an open space.

Right *A map of Moorfields and the surrounding area.*

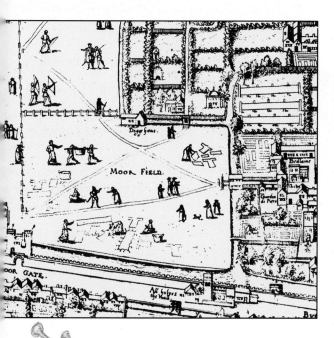

Faced with having to live in the open for some time, Londoners quickly showed their ingenuity. Moorfields soon became a mass of tents and huts. Temporary housing was made out of almost anything that came to hand. Sheets became tents. Even scorched timbers salvaged from the ruins were used to build shelters.

Within a few days the bustle of the city had recreated itself out on Moorfields. Tradespeople set up shop in tents, inns opened in huts and in the open air. It amazed visitors how quickly the people of London recovered from the terrible disaster.

Below *The camp at Moorfields.*

FUTURE PLANS

London had been devastated by the fire. It would take a great effort to rebuild it into a thriving capital city. Just as King Charles had been a driving force in the fire-fighting, so he took a hand in the building of a new London.

On September 10 he called in Sir Christopher Wren, a great **architect**, to help with the plans for a new London.

Below *Charles II and Wren discuss plans for a "new" city.*

It was decided that efforts should be made to prevent such a disastrous fire from breaking out ever again. Building laws were passed that imposed strict new rules. No wooden buildings were to be allowed. All houses and stores had to be constructed of either brick or stone. The narrow, winding streets of old London were swept away. Important streets were straightened, and even back streets were made much wider than they had been.

Wren and another architect, John Evelyn, produced detailed plans for a completely new road system.

Below *People from all over the country sent money for the people made homeless in the fire. This receipt, for 53 shillings, is from Cowfold in Sussex.*

This Boy is in Memmory Put up for the late Fire of LONDON Occasion'd by the Sin of Gluttony 1666

Above *A small statue erected at "Pye Corner" (now Pie Corner), Smithfields, to mark the spot where the fire was finally halted.*

Received the 26th: day of November 1666. of Mr. Thomas Lintott returned from Cowfold in Sussex the Summe of fifty three shillings & Nine pence which was collected in the said Parish on the Fast Day, being the 10th day of October 1666. towards the Relief of those Persons who have been great Sufferers by the late Sad Fire within the City of London. I say Recd. by order of the Lord Major.

Sa: Kendall.

Above *The old St. Paul's Cathedral as it appeared in 1620.*

Above *Wren's plan for the new St. Paul's Cathedral.*

These plans included broad **piazzas** and streets. However, the architects met with opposition. The city merchants pointed out that the main business of London was trade and government. They insisted that the city be rebuilt as swiftly as possible with the buildings conveniently close together.

So it was that new buildings began to rise along the remains of the old main streets. However, the King and Wren were able to keep the new laws about the use of stone and brick.

The design of many new buildings was entrusted to Wren. In all he was to be responsible for building 51 new churches, and a magnificent new St. Paul's Cathedral, which was begun in 1675. The great domed cathedral and many of the churches are still landmarks in London today.

In 1667 King Charles laid the first stone of the new Royal Exchange. Many other important new buildings were begun in that year. By 1669 the city was on its way to being completely rebuilt.

The vast crowds had left Moorfields for new homes on old sites. Trade, industry and government had almost returned to normal.

In 1671 the Corporation of London began the construction of the Monument to commemorate the Great Fire. It was decided that the Monument should take the form of a column, which Wren was asked to design.

The magnificent column he designed can still be seen. It is built of Portland stone and is 61.5 m (200 ft) tall — the distance it stands from the site of John Farynor's bakery where the fire began. The column is topped by a flaming urn, representing the flames of the fire. A spiral staircase runs up inside the pillar. You can climb up these stairs to the top of the Monument and gaze at the city that rose from the ashes of the fire of London.

Above *The Monument.*

Left *London thirty years after the fire, with all the rebuilding complete.*

GLOSSARY

Acrid   Unpleasant and strong smelling.

Apprentice   A young person who lives with a master craftsman to learn a trade.

Architect   Someone who designs buildings.

Daub   A type of plaster used on walls during the seventeenth century.

Faggots   Bundles of dry wood used for lighting fires.

Ferryman   One of the men who owned small boats and earned a living by rowing people up and down the Thames.

Fire-break   A strip of land kept clear to prevent the spread of fire.

Fleet River   A narrow river that flows through the center of London. At the time of the fire it flowed through the streets into the Thames. It is now entirely underground.

Guinea   A gold coin worth about one English pound. In 1666 this was a great deal of money.

Lord Mayor   The leader of the government of the City of London. At the time of the fire the Lord Mayor was Sir Thomas Bludworth.

Master Goldsmith   A senior goldsmith who has passed all the tests in making gold jewelry and is allowed to work as a goldsmith.

Militia   A group of citizens given military training.

Piazza   A large square in a city, modeled after the squares in Italian cities.

Privy Council   A body of advisors to the King or Queen.

Royal Exchange   A trading center in the middle of London where merchants from all over Europe met to set up deals and buy goods.

Squirt   Fire-fighting equipment used in 1666. It consisted of a nozzle held by two men, and a pump worked by a third. A squirt could shoot 4.5 liters (5.6 gal) of water at a burning building from some distance away.

Tinder   Very dry material, especially wood, that burns easily.

Trained Bands   Londoners, trained in the use of weapons, who could be called upon to defend the city in time of war.

Warehouses   Large buildings, found beside docks, where goods are stored either before being loaded onto ships or after unloading.

Watchmen   Men paid by the city of London to walk around the streets at night to keep a watch for criminals and other trouble.

Wharves   Landing platforms built along the edges of a river, for loading and unloading of goods from boats.

BOOKS TO READ

Here are some other books you may wish to read about the Fire of London and life in the times of King Charles II.

Disastrous Fires by George S. Fichter. Franklin Watts, 1981.
Great Disasters by Andrew Langley. The Bookwright Press, 1986.
The Great Fire of London by David A. Weiss. Crown Publishers, 1968.
Plague and Fire: The Story of London by Peter Gray. McGraw-Hill, 1967.

FURTHER INFORMATION

Many of the places connected with the Fire of London still exist. The new St. Paul's Cathedral and other churches and buildings by Sir Christopher Wren can easily be visited.

The street plan of central London today is very similar to that of London in 1666, and it is possible to follow the course of the fire.

It is interesting to visit the Monument, which was built to commemorate the fire. It stands beside the Thames, on the north bank near London Bridge, where the fire first broke out. You can climb to the top by way of the spiral staircase inside.

The Museum of London has a special display about the fire. Called "The Great Fire Experience," it consists of a model of London as it was in 1666, with vivid sound and light effects recreating the fire. This is shown continuously throughout the day.

Index

Page numbers that refer to pictures are in **bold**.

Bakery, the King's 12, 13
Bludworth, Sir Thomas 14, 15
Botolph Lane 6, **7**
Bridewell 20
Buildings,
    construction of 11
    new laws 28

Charles II, King **10**, 19, 20, 21, 22, 23, **26**, 28

Docks, the 8, 9

Farynor, John 12, 29
Ferrymen 6
Fire, the **5**, 7, **12**, **13**, **14**, **15**, **18**, **19**
    control of 23
    damage caused by 23
    deaths due to 12, 24
    escaping 4-5, 6
    the start of 11, 12
Fire equipment 5, **22**, 23
Fire-fighters 14, 21, 22, 26

Fire Posts 19
Fleet River 20

London,
    rebuilding of 26, 27, **28**

Merchants 8, 28
Monument, the 29
Moorfields camp 24, 25, 29

Parliament 10
Pepys, Samuel 14, **15**
Philpot Lane 6, **7**
Pudding Lane 7, 12, **13**

Royal Exchange 8, **9**, 20, 28

St. Paul's Cathedral 20, 28

Thames River 6, 8, 17
Trained bands 5, 19

Warehouses 16
Watchmen 14, **19**
Whitehall 10, 14
Wren, Sir Christopher **26**, 28

Acknowledgments

The publishers would like to thank the following for providing the photographs in this book: BBC Hulton Picture Library 17, 18, 19 (above), 22 (below), 26, 28 (right); The Bridgeman Art Library 6, 7 (below), 8-9, 14-15, 29 (right); E.T. Archive 22 (middle both); The Mansell Collection COVER, 7 (above), 9 (above); Mary Evans Picture Library 11 (above), 16, 28 (left), 29 (left); Michael Holford 10 (above); The Museum of London 15 (both), 19 (above), 25 (inset), 27 (both). The artwork on page 11 is by Stan North.